Every Kid's Guide to
Thinking and Learning

Written by
JOY BERRY

CHILDRENS PRESS ®
CHICAGO

About the Author and Publisher

Joy Berry's mission in life is to help families cope with everyday problems and to help children become competent, responsible, happy individuals. To achieve her goal, she has written over two hundred self-help books for children from birth through age twelve. Her work revolutionized children's publishing by providing families with practical, how-to, living skills information that was previously unavailable in children's books.

Joy gathered a dedicated team of experts, including psychologists, educators, child developmentalists, writers, editors, designers, and artists, to form her publishing company and to help produce her work.

The company, Living Skills Press, produces thoroughly researched books and audio-visual materials that successfully combine humor and education to teach subjects ranging from how to clean a bedroom to how to resolve problems and get along with other people.

Managing Editor: Ellen Klarberg
Copy Editor: Kate Dickey
Contributing Editors: Libby Byers, Nancy Cochran, Maureen Dryden, Yona Flemming, Kathleen Mohr, Susan Motycka
Editorial Assistant: Sandy Passarino

Art Director: Laurie Westdahl
Design: Abigail Johnston, Laurie Westdahl
Production: Abigail Johnston, Caroline Rennard
Illustrations designed by: Bartholomew
Inker: Linda Hanney
Colorer: Linda Hanney
Composition: Curt Chelin

Your brain is an important part of you. It performs many wonderful functions. All these functions are important in thinking and learning.

In **EVERY KID'S GUIDE TO THINKING AND LEARNING**, you will find out about the following:

- thinking,
- curiosity,
- learning styles,
- teaching styles,
- the best styles for you,
- knowing, and
- remembering.

T*hinking* is an important function of your brain.

Thinking is using your mind
- to form thoughts, ideas, opinions, and
- to make decisions.

Thinking is something your brain does all the time.

ALL DAY LONG...

ALL NIGHT LONG...

Sometimes you think without realizing that you are thinking.

This is called *involuntary thinking*.

Activities such as breathing, chewing, swallowing, and walking are results of involuntary thinking.

Sometimes you cause yourself to think.

This is called *voluntary thinking*.

Activities such as solving problems, studying, and reading are results of voluntary thinking.

Curiosity is another important function of your brain.

Curiosity is
- wondering and
- wanting to know about something that is strange, new, or interesting.

Curiosity is what motivates you to learn.

Learning is another important function of your brain.

Learning is
- gaining new knowledge and
- gaining new skills.

Although you have learned a great deal of information and skills, there is always more you can learn.

Learning can happen in one of two ways.

1. You can learn on your own.

2. Other people can help you learn.

There are several ways to learn on your own. One way is to *observe* something.

When you observe something, you
- look at it closely or
- watch it carefully.

Learning this way is called ***learning through observation.***

Another way to learn on your own is to *experience* something.

When you experience something, you
- touch it,
- handle it, and
- use it.

You can also taste it and smell it if it is appropriate
to do so.

Learning this way is called *learning through
experience.*

Another way to learn on your own is to **talk** about something.

When you talk about something, you
- ask questions about it,
- listen to the answers to your questions, and
- share your thoughts and feelings about it.

Learning this way is called *learning through verbalization.*

Another way to learn on your own is to **read** about something.

You can read books, magazines, pamphlets, and newspapers that can be

- purchased or
- borrowed from your school or community library.

Learning this way is called *learning through reading.*

The various ways you can learn on your own are called *learning styles.*

Learning styles include
- learning through observation,
- learning through experience,
- learning through verbalization, and
- learning through reading.

Other people can help you learn by *teaching* you whatever you need or want to know.

When people teach you something, they share
information that helps you learn.

There are several ways people can teach you.

Verbal teaching is one way you can be taught.

Verbal teaching happens when people share
information with you by talking to you.

Teaching through demonstration is another way you can be taught.

Teaching through demonstration happens when
people show you
- how to do something or
- how something works.

Teaching by example is another way you can be taught.

When people teach by example, they do something and then encourage you to
- watch them and
- copy their behavior.

Motivational teaching is another way you can be taught.

Motivational teaching happens when people
- expose you to a new subject and
- stimulate your curiosity about it.

The various ways you can be taught are called *teaching styles.*

Teaching styles include
- verbal teaching,
- teaching through demonstration,
- teaching by example, and
- motivational teaching.

To learn everything you need to learn, you should know which learning and teaching styles work best for you. You can find this out by following these four steps:

Step 1. Be aware of the various learning and teaching styles.

Step 2. Try each learning and teaching style.

Step 3. Pay attention to how well you respond to each learning and teaching style.

Answer these questions:

- How much do I enjoy this style?
- How well do I learn with this style?

Step 4. Use the learning and teaching styles that work best for you.

It is important for you and your parents to find out which learning and teaching styles work best for you.

Once you and your parents know which styles work best for you, it is important that you communicate this information to the administrators or counselors at your school. Hopefully, these people will assign you to appropriate classrooms. An appropriate classroom will have a teacher and program that utilizes the learning and teaching styles that work best for you.

Once you learn something, you know it.

Knowing is another important function of the brain. Knowing is

- understanding and
- being certain of the facts or truth about something.

Knowing makes it possible for you to live your life
more intelligently and responsibly.

Remembering is another important function of the brain.

Remembering is recalling something you already know.

Remembering helps you put the things you already know into use.

Your brain is a wonderful part of you. It makes it possible for you to

- think,
- wonder,
- learn,
- know, and
- remember.